Basic Map Reading

Keith Gillard

*Chief Examiner for the
WJEC Certificate of Education,
Geography*

Longman

Longman Group UK Limited
Longman House, Burnt Mill, Harlow,
Essex, CM20 2JE, England and
Associated Companies throughout the
World.

First published 1990
ISBN 0 582 036879

Set in Best-set Typesetter Ltd
Produced by Longman Group (F.E.) Limited
Printed in Hong Kong

The Ordnance Survey map extacts are
reproduced with the permission of the Controller
of Her Majesty's Stationery office. © Crown Copyright
reserved. 1989

Acknowledgements

We are grateful to the following for
permission to reproduce photographs:
Aerofilms, pages 38, 41 *above*; British
Rail – InterCity, page 16; British
Waterways Board, page 17 (2); J Allan
Cash, pages 13, 15 (2), 20 (3), 22, 26
(3), 27 *above*, 27 *left*, 28 (3), 29 *centre*,
29 *below*, 34, 41 *below*; Peter Dazeley,
page 27 *below*; Anne Gilliam E.O ©;
G.S.F. Picture Library, page 37; Holt
Studios Ltd, pages 25, 29 *above*; The
Post Office, page 27 *right*; Youth
Hostels Association, page 21 (photo:
D. Higgs).
Cover: 125 InterCity train crossing a
viaduct. Photo: British Rail-InterCity.

The author wishes to thank Mr Graham
Woosuam, WJEC Chief Examiner,
for his constant advice and support
without which this book would not
have been possible.

Contents

1 What is a map?

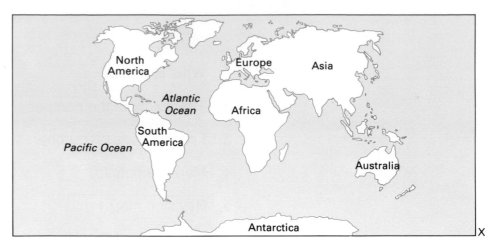

Figure 1

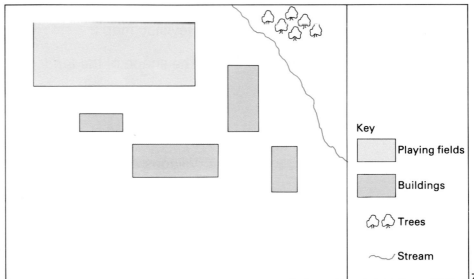

The three diagrams above are all maps. Map X is a map of the world, Map Y is a map of Britain and Map Z is a map of a school.

1 Copy out the following sentences choosing the correct phrases in the brackets to complete them.

A map is always drawn (larger/smaller) than the full size area.
A map is always seen from (above/below/the side).
A map shows (everything that can be seen from above/all the biggest features/only what the map maker wants to show).

2 Name an extra feature that you would have wanted to add to each of these three maps.

On Map X the world has been reduced in size to fit the map. The same has happened with the map of Britain and the map of the school.

3 Which of these three areas has been reduced **a** the most? **b** the least?

Figure 2

The map of the school contains buildings, trees, playing fields and a stream. They are shown by different shapes called **map symbols**.

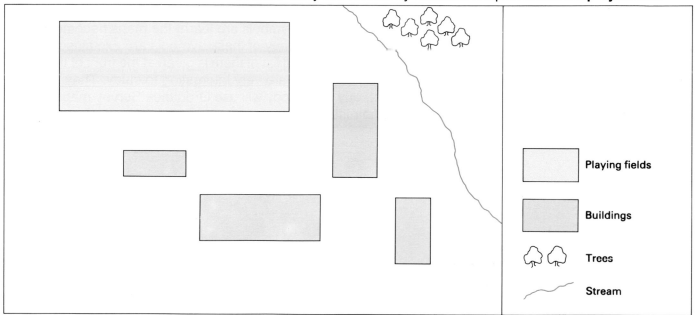

Playing fields

Buildings

Trees

Stream

Figure 3

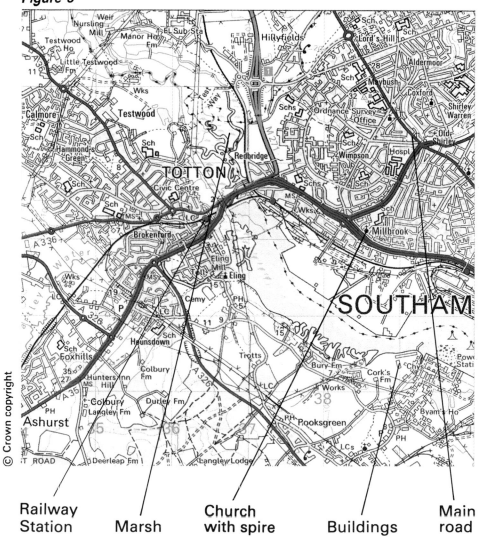

© Crown copyright

Railway Station

Marsh

Church with spire

Buildings

Main road

Each symbol together with its meaning is shown beside the map. This is a **key**.

4 Why do you think symbols are used on maps?
5 Copy the map of the school and its key into your exercise book.
6 Make up symbols for a tennis court and a path. Add these to your map and to your key.

Many of the maps in this book are **Ordnance Survey** maps. For the past two centuries the Ordnance Survey has produced detailed maps for all parts of Britain. As you can see, they use many different kinds of symbols.

5

These symbols help people to understand what the land looks like and what is found on it.

At first glance Ordnance Survey maps seem to be crowded with symbols. But once these symbols are learnt the maps become very clear and simple to use. Many of these symbols are explained in the early part of this book. A full list of them is given at the front of the book.

Ordnance Survey maps are very interesting to study. They are also very useful. Nearly everybody will use Ordnance Survey maps at some time during their life.

Figure 4

7 Look at the drawings and explain how these people might use an Ordnance Survey map.

8 Find out the name we give to a book of maps. (Unravel the letters SALTA to check your answer!)

9 Copy out the following paragraph and fill in the missing words.

The whole of B＿＿＿＿＿＿＿ has been mapped by the O＿＿＿＿＿＿＿＿ Survey. The maps they draw are always s＿＿＿＿＿＿ than the area they show. They contain s＿＿＿＿＿＿ which help people to understand more about the land. The meanings of these symbols are shown in a k＿＿.

2 The points of the compass

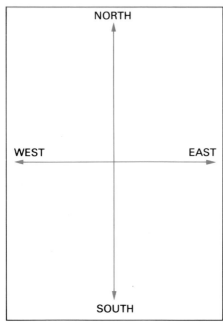

Figure 1

It is often necessary to say where one thing is in relation to another. When laying a table we put the fork to the left of the plate and the knife to the right. You could describe the position of your nose as being above your mouth but below your eyes. When describing places on the Earth's surface we do not say left, right, above or below but rather west, east, north and south. These are the directions used most and they are often referred to as the **four main points of the compass** (see Figure 1).

There are also directions between the four main points of the compass. The most important of these are shown in Figure 2.

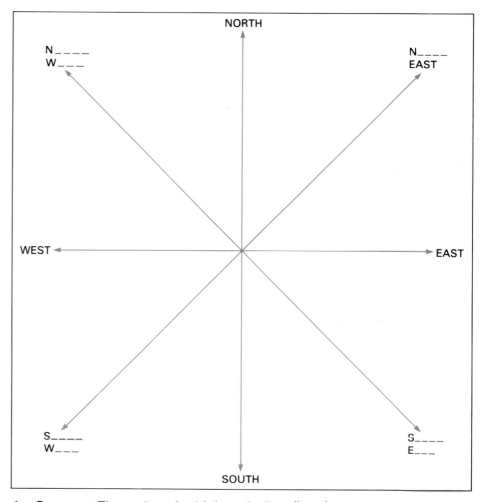

Figure 2

1 Copy out Figure 2 and add the missing directions.

The map below shows the route taken to school by two girls.

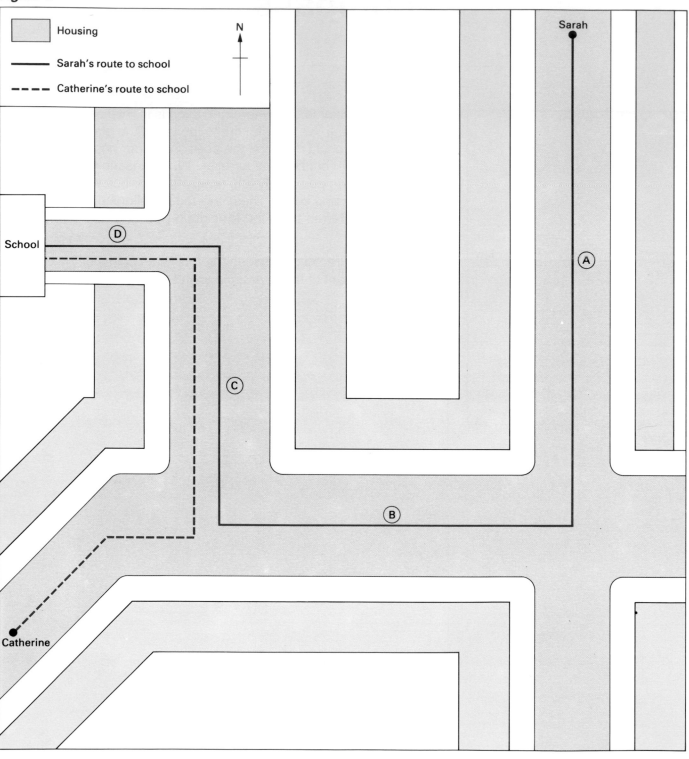

Figure 3

2 In what direction is Sarah walking at **A**, **B**, **C**, and **D**?

3 Catherine's route to school is shown by a dashed line. On her journey she walks in four different directions. Which are they?

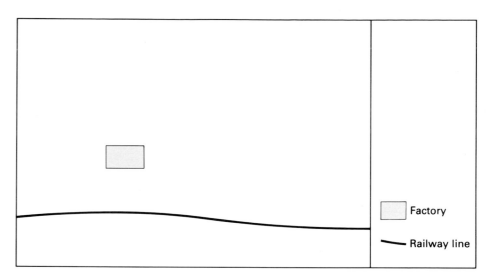

Figure 4

4 Copy Figure 4 into your exercise book. With the help of the full list at the front of the book, find out the symbols for a railway station, a church with a tower, a post office and a wood. Draw the railway station symbol to the south of the factory and the small wood symbol to the west of it. Now draw other symbols to place the post office to the south-west of the railway station and the church with tower to the north-east of the factory. Complete the key at the side of your map.

5 Look at the map of the British Isles and copy out the following sentences, filling in the blanks.

Figure 5

Cardiff lies to the w_ _ _ _ of London.
Belfast is n_ _ _ _ _ _-w_ _ _ _ of London.
Edinburgh is n_ _ _ _ _ _-e_ _ _ _ of Belfast.
Cardiff if s_ _ _ _ _ _-e_ _ _ _ of Dublin.
Dublin is north-west of C_ _ _ _ _ _ _ _.
Edinburgh is n_ _ _ _ _ _ of Cardiff.

3 Fixing places by numbers

Most Ordnance Survey maps are criss-crossed by straight blue lines. These are **grid lines** and are used to find places on the map. As you can see, each grid line has been given a number.

Figure 1

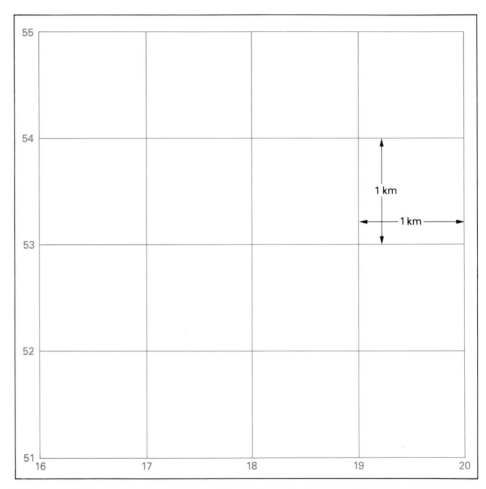

These grid lines form squares. The sides of these grid squares are 1 kilometre in length.

To identify a grid square the grid lines on the left and the bottom must both be numbered.

Figure 2

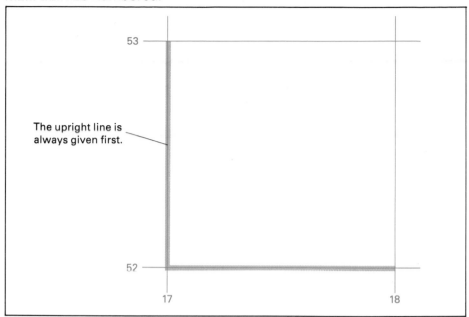

This makes the letter L. The left hand (upright) grid line is 17 and the bottom grid line is 52. So the number of this grid square is 1752. This is a **four figure grid reference**.

Figure 3

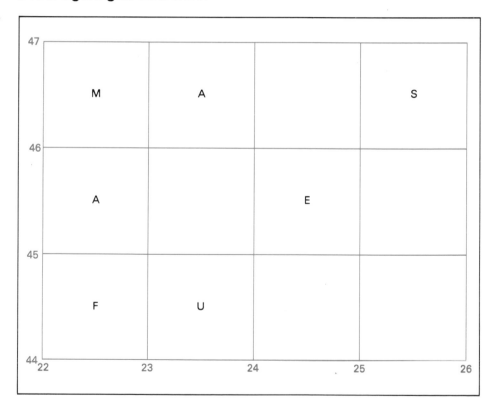

1 Copy Figure 3 into your exercise book. Place letter P in grid square 2446, R in 2345 and N in 2444. What sentence have you made?

Figure 4

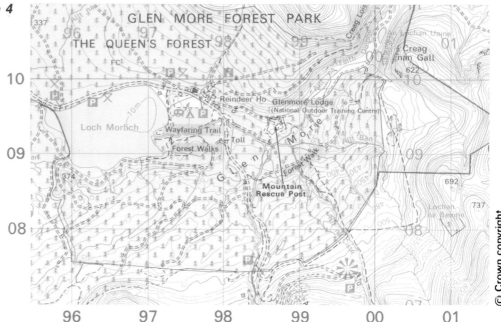

2 Why would a parachutist not wish to land in grid square 9609?

3 Name a grid square where camping is popular.

4 In which grid square is the mountain rescue post? 9808, 9909 or 9809?

5 Why is it more expensive to drive in grid square 9809 than elsewhere on the map?

If the exact position of a symbol has to be pinpointed, a **six figure grid reference** is needed. To do this you must imagine the distance between each grid line is divided into ten equal parts. On the example this has been done for you.(Such small divisions do not appear on real maps!)

The railway station lies somewhere between grid line 17 and 18. As you can see from the diagram it lies 8/10 (eight-tenths) of the way across. This is said to be 17**8**. The railway station also lies somewhere between grid line 52 and 53. This time it is only 6/10 (six-tenths) of the way between the two lines. The second part of the grid reference is therefore 52**6**. If the two parts are joined together a six figure grid reference is made – 17**8**52**6**.

6 With the help of Figure 4, copy out the following paragraph and complete the blanks in it.

Last summer two boys, Rajiv and Tom, cycled to Loch M_ _ _ _ _ _ _ _. They stopped at the parking area at 958_ _ _ _ to admire the beautiful loch. An hour later they continued their journey along the minor road to the youth hostel at 976_ _ _ _. A friend of theirs, Janine, was staying at a nearby camping site at _ _ _ _ _ _ _ _. On Sunday the three met at the small church at 978_ _ _. In the afternoon they decided to go hiking to the south-west of the loch where they climbed to 374 metres at _ _ _ _ _ _ _ _. Unfortunately Rajiv slipped and twisted his ankle. Hours later he was brought back by the mountain rescue team from _ _ _ _ _ _ _ _.

Figure 5

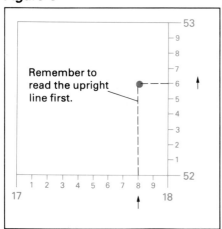

Remember to read the upright line first.

4 Map symbols (a)

Road symbols

Britain's main cities are linked by **motorways** which provide fast, direct travel between them. The photograph shows part of the M62 in North Humberside.

Figure 1

Traffic joins or leaves a motorway by using **slip roads** like the one in the photograph. These slip roads are found at **junctions** which are given special numbers. **Service areas** have been built at intervals along motorways. Drivers use them to buy petrol or food. Some even have bedrooms.

Figure 2

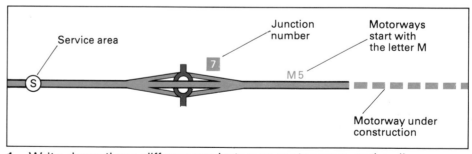

1   Write down three differences between motorways and ordinary roads (the photograph will help you).
2   The motorway in the photograph has no sharp bends. Why do you think most motorways are built this way?

Motorways are only one type of road. The other types are **main roads, secondary roads** and **minor roads**. Main roads are fairly wide and carry a lot of traffic. Most secondary roads are not quite as wide, but they too have a good surface. Minor roads may be narrow and have sharp bends.

Figure 3

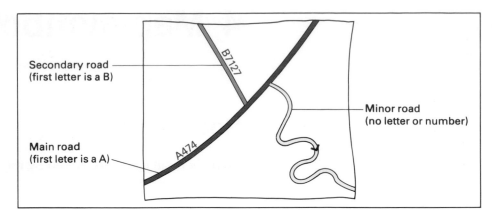

Secondary road
(first letter is a B)

Minor road
(no letter or number)

Main road
(first leter is a A)

The minor road in Figure 3 has a black arrow. This symbol tells us how steep the road is. One arrow means that the road has a **gradient** between 1:5 and 1:7. A gradient 1:5 means that the land rises or falls by one metre for every five metres along the road. This is shown in Figure 4.

Figure 4

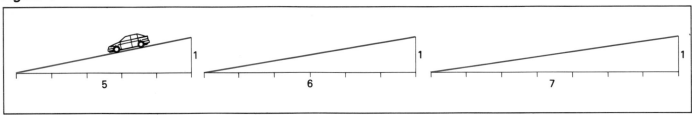

Two arrows mean the gradient is even steeper than 1:5.

3 Which is steeper, 1:5 or 1:7?
4 Find out the numbers of the nearest main road and nearest secondary road to your school.
5 Find out the speed limit on a motorway (in miles per hour).

Figure 5

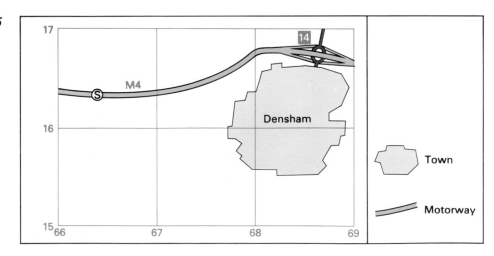

6 Why has this motorway not been built in a straight line?
7 At what junction should a motorist leave the M4 to visit Densham? (Give its number.)
8 Give the six figure grid reference of a place where motorists buy petrol and have a meal.

Railway symbols

Figure 6

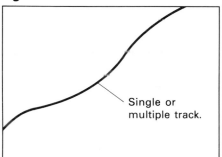

Single or multiple track.

There are many **railway** symbols too.

This type of railway line has one or more tracks. Both passengers and goods are carried on these lines. Britain's major cities are linked by Inter City lines, on which trains travel quickly and make few stops.

Figure 7

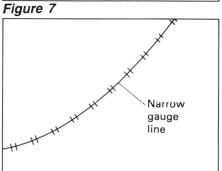

Narrow gauge line

The distance between these tracks is narrower than those of main railway lines. These narrow lines usually carry steam trains and many of them are very popular with tourists.

Figure 8

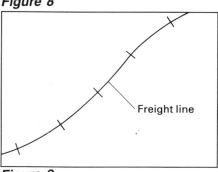

Freight line

A freight line carries goods trains only. A freight line may lead off the main line to a factory or port.

Trains have steel wheels. To stop them from slipping on the steel rails the gradient of the track is kept as level as possible.

If there is a slight rise in the land a **cutting** is made through which the line passes.

Figure 9

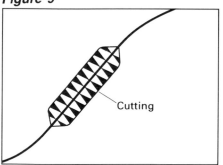

Cutting

If there is a slight dip the land is built up to form an **embankment**.

Figure 10

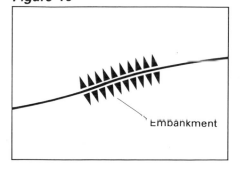

Embankment

Three symbols are used to show railway stations on Ordnance Survey maps. The largest is the **principal station** which is usually found in large cities.

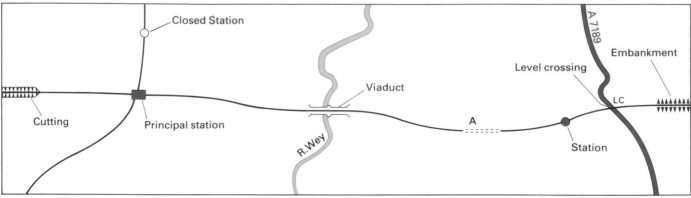

Figure 11

9 How many stations have been closed in Figure 11?
10 The land at **A** is too high for a cutting. What did the railway engineer build instead? (The full list of symbols will help you.)
11 What has been built in Figure 11 to allow the A7189 road to cross the railway?

Figure 12

If a railway has to cross a valley then a bridge must be built.

If the railway bridge is made up of several arches then it is called a **viaduct**.

Figure 13

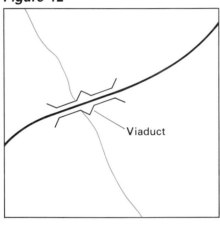

12 How many railway stations are there on the map?
13 What has been built between Newhaven and Bishopstone stations to keep the gradient of the railway line as gentle as possible? What has been built on the other side of Bishopstone station?
14 If you went by train from Newhaven to Bishopstone, in which direction would you be travelling?
15 Apart from the main track, what other type of railway line is found near to Newhaven?

Symbols for rivers, streams and canals

Figure 14

Streams are shown by thin blue lines. **Rivers** are wider and deeper than streams and so are shown by thicker blue lines. Streams and rivers are **natural** features; they have many bends.

Canals are man-made waterways. They are much straighter.

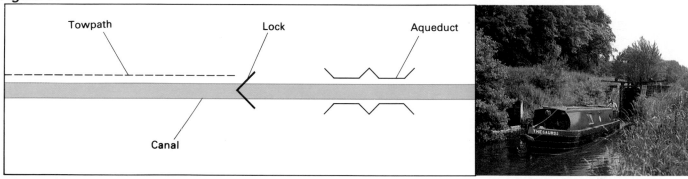

Figure 15

The arrow in the above diagram is the symbol for a **lock**. A lock is a small stretch of the canal enclosed by gates. Barges use locks to move to higher or lower levels of the canal.

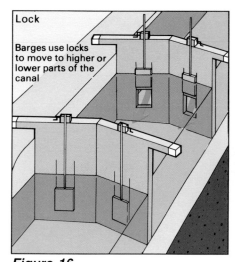

Figure 16

16 Copy out the following paragraph choosing the correct words from the box underneath.

Barges are a s_ _ _ _ but cheap way of carrying goods. In the past barges sailed along British c_ _ _ _ _ _ carrying bulky goods such as c_ _ _ _ and iron ore. Competition from faster road and r_ _ _ _ transport led to many canals becoming disused. However, in some parts of the world canals are still very important for carrying h_ _ _ _ _ goods.

   In Britain the number of p_ _ _ _ _ _ _ _ craft has greatly increased in recent years. This has led to the re-opening of many d_ _ _ _ _ _ _ canals.

canals	coal	disused	heavy
pleasure		rail	slow

5 Revision map 1

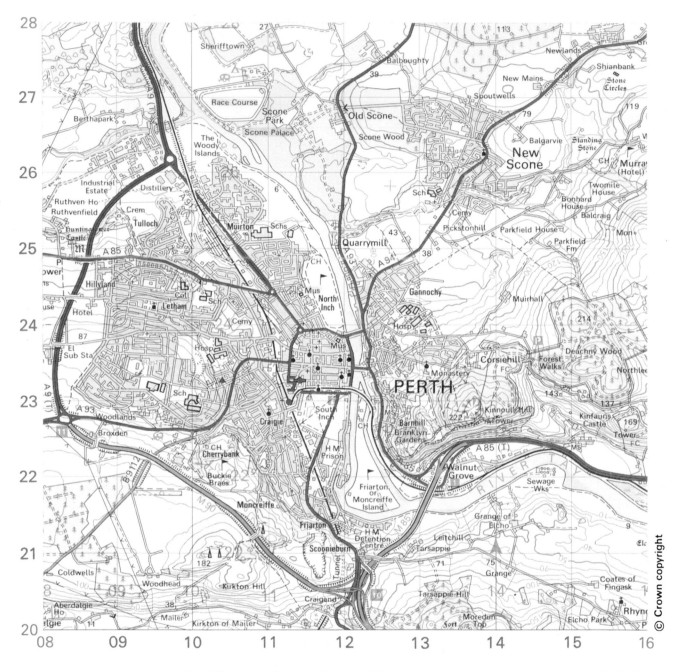

© Crown copyright

1 What are the numbers of the two motorways to the south of Perth?
2 Why do you think these two motorways were not built in a straight line across the map?
3 Name the four different types of road in square 0922.
4 How many road bridges cross the River Tay?
5 Why are there so many roads in square 1220?
6 What has been built in 0926 to protect the railway from flooding?
7 Name a square where you would expect to find many freight trains.
8 What is the six figure grid reference for Perth railway station?

6 Map symbols (b)

Coastal symbols

The coast is that part of the land which lies next to the sea. Some coasts are rocky and may have towering cliffs. Other parts of the coast have sandy beaches which are crowded with holiday makers during the summer months.

Some of the most important coastal symbols are shown below.

Figure 1

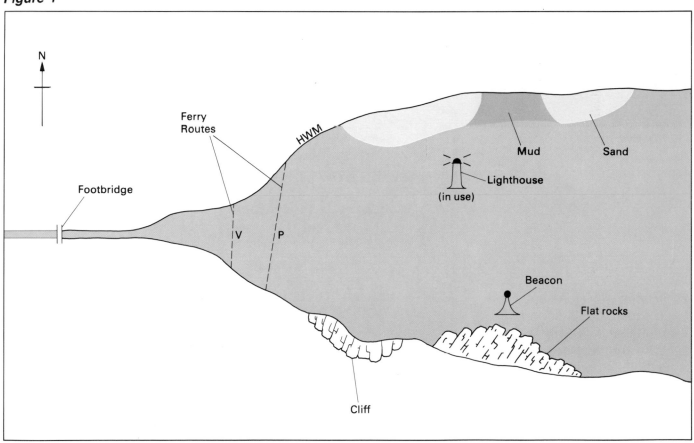

The coastline itself is shown as a black line. This is the **high water mark (HWM)** which the sea reaches at high tide. Inland from the **footbridge** the river is edged by blue lines. This means that the level of the river does not rise and fall with the tide. The river is no longer 'tidal'.

Two **ferry** routes are shown. Ferries are ships used to take people on short journeys (**P**). The letter **V** means that the ferry can also carry vehicles.

Rocks and sandbanks near the coast are dangerous to ships. **Beacons** and **lighthouses** have been built to warn their captains.

Figure 2

Lighthouse

Beacon

1 An **estuary** is the tidal part of the river. Copy Figure 1, which shows an estuary, into your exercise book. Print the letter A where it might be dangerous to walk. State why it is also dangerous to sail north of the lighthouse and south of the beacon.

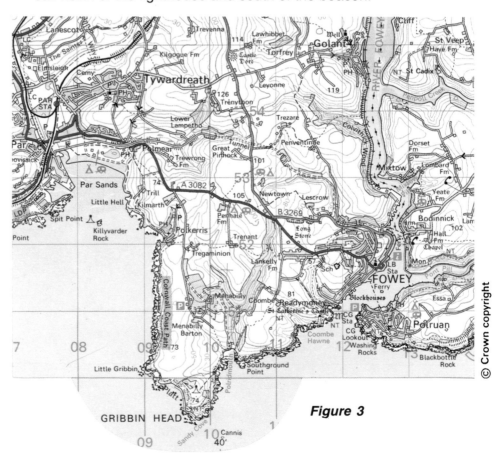

Figure 3

© Crown copyright

2 In what way is the coastline in square 0853 different from that in 0951?
3 Why are there beacons at **a** 082524 and **b** 098498?
4 State four ways in which we can tell that ships sail in the Fowey area.

5 If you sailed from Gribbin Head to Fowey, in which direction would you be heading?
6 Where could your ship shelter to avoid a storm?

Tourist symbols

Ordnance Survey maps contain special information for holidaymakers and day trippers. Many of these tourist symbols are coloured blue.

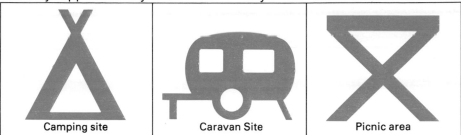

Figure 4

Camping site | Caravan Site | Picnic area

Most day trippers travel by car so **parking areas** are very important. Places where tourists can obtain information about the surrounding area are also useful. They are called **information centres**.

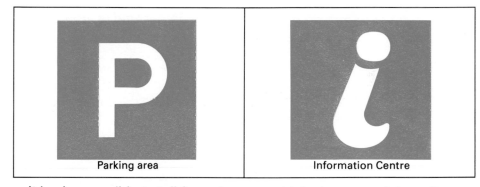

Figure 5

Parking area | Information Centre

It is also possible to tell from the map which places are interesting and worth a visit.

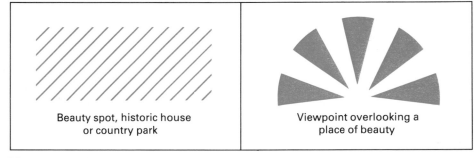

Beauty spot, historic house or country park | Viewpoint overlooking a place of beauty

Figure 6

Young people enjoy visiting the countryside but usually cannot afford to stay in hotels. **Youth hostels** have been built to provide food and a place to sleep at reasonable prices.

Figure 7

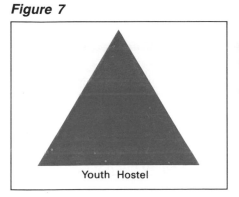

Youth Hostel

The **National Trust** owns many famous houses, castles and wildlife centres. Such places are visited by large numbers of tourists.

Figure 8

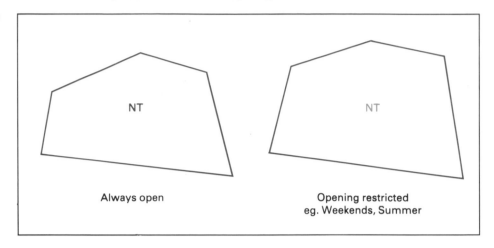

Always open

Opening restricted
eg. Weekends, Summer

A much larger kind of area used by tourists is a **national park**.

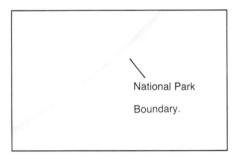

National Park

Boundary.

Figure 9

Figure 9 shows part of the Lake District National Park. This is one of the ten national parks in England and Wales. As you can see, national parks are places of great beauty. Most of them are in the mountainous parts of the country. These areas are protected by but not owned by the government.

Figure 10

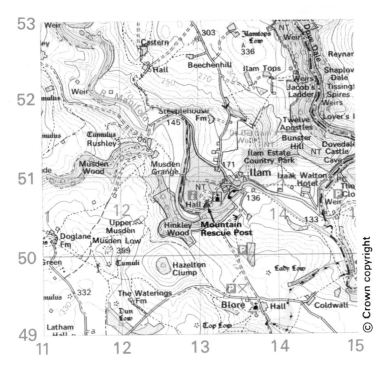

Map B

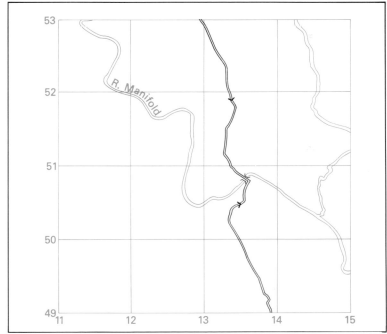

Map B is a simple sketch map of the area shown in the Ordnance Survey map.

7 Copy this sketch map into your exercise book. Mark on it, using the correct symbols, the youth hostel, the three parking areas and Ilam Estate Country Park.

8 Mark with a letter A two places where driving your car might be difficult.

9 Draw in the national park boundary.

10 Who owns Hinkley Wood?

11 Where could you stay overnight?

Woodland symbols

A thousand years ago much of Britain was covered with **woodland**. Most of this woodland has now been cleared to make way for towns, factories and farms.

The woods that remain are shown by the symbol in Figure 11. This is **mixed woodland**.

Figure 11

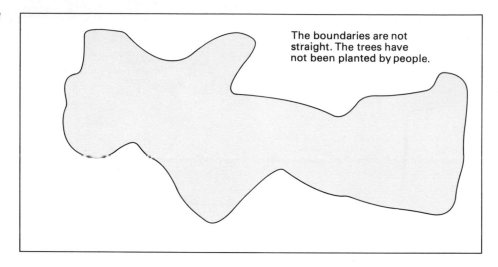

The boundaries are not straight. The trees have not been planted by people.

In many parts of upland Britain trees are planted by the **Forestry Commission**. They include pine, fir and spruce trees which are able to withstand the wet and cold climate of the uplands. These hardy trees only take about twenty-five years to grow.

Figure 12

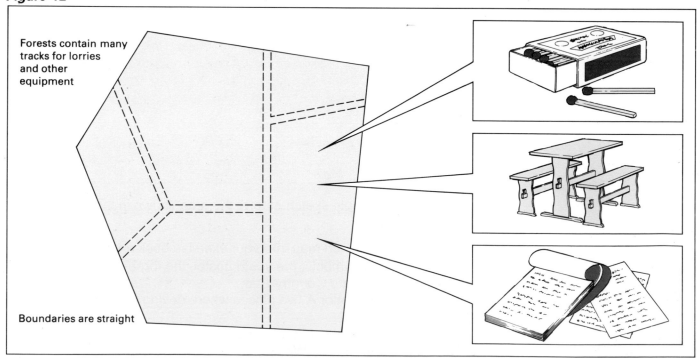

Forests contain many tracks for lorries and other equipment

Boundaries are straight

12 With the help of Figure 12, state three uses for Forestry Commission timber.

Figure 13 shows another group of trees planted by people.

Figure 13

Orchard

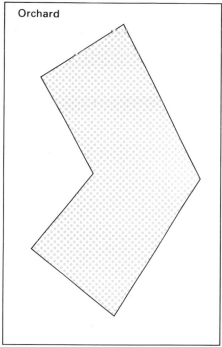

Figure 14

Spruce tree

Oak tree

This is an **orchard** where trees are grown for fruit, for example, apples and pears.

13 Figure 14 shows drawings of a spruce tree and an oak tree. Copy these two trees into your exercise book. Under each tree write out the paragraph filling in the blank spaces from the words in the box.

Most of the trees grown by the Forestry _____ are conifers. A _____ tree is one example of a conifer. It is a _____ tree with needles rather than leaves. This helps it to survive _____ winters. A spruce tree takes about _____ years to grow. Much of the timber from conifers is used to make _____.

Most of Britain's _____ woodland is made up of deciduous trees such as elm and _____. Deciduous trees shed their leaves in _____ and cannot survive a harsh climate. They take many years to grow, sometimes _____. The timber from deciduous trees is very strong and may be used to make _____ furniture.

| 25 Commission paper | centuries expensive natural |
| harsh spruce coniferous | oak winter |

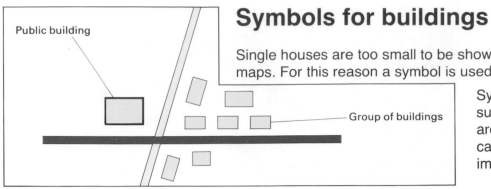

Figure 15

Symbols for buildings

Single houses are too small to be shown on 1:50 000 Ordnance Survey maps. For this reason a symbol is used to show a group of buildings.

Symbols for important **public buildings** such as libraries and hospitals are edged by thick black lines. In some cases letters are used to indicate important buildings.

Chapels and **churches** are shown by symbols which tell us whether they have a tower, a spire or neither.

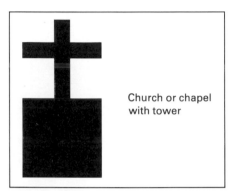

Church or chapel with tower

Figure 16

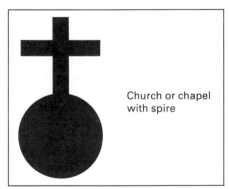

Church or chapel with spire

Figure 17

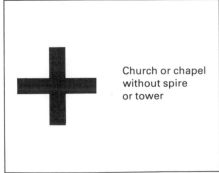

Church or chapel without spire or tower

Figure 18

26

14 What do each of the letters in the four drawings stand for? (The full list of symbols will help you.)

Figure 19

TH
CH

PH
P

Symbols for general features

Electricity is sent around the country by a system of cables. These are supported by tall pylons like those in Figure 20 to form **electricity transmission lines.**

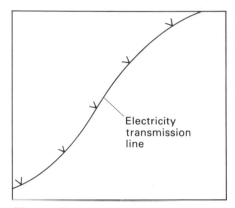

Figure 20

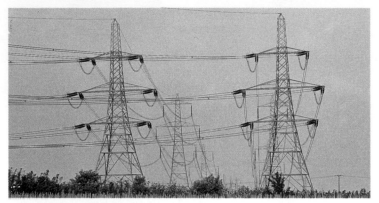

Rocks from **quarries** may be used to build houses. Some rocks such as limestone are important raw materials needed by industry.

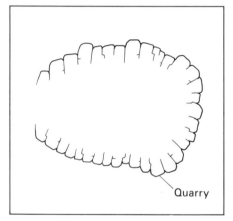

Figure 21

Spoil heaps containing waste from both homes and factories are shown on maps. Figure 22 shows one example in a coal-mining area.

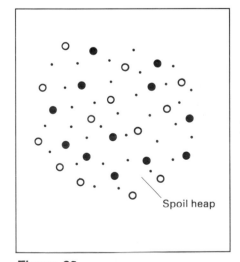

Figure 22

Some farms have areas under glass where fruit and vegetables are grown. As the **glasshouses** can be heated, the plants in them can grow throughout the year.

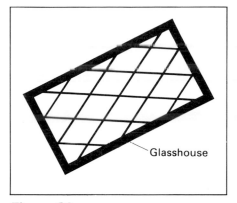

Glasshouse

Figure 23

Television Masts are usually found on higher ground where it is easier for them to transmit signals to our television sets.

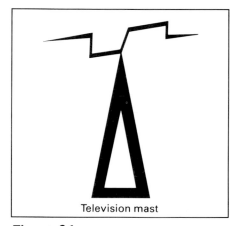

Television mast

Figure 24

Marshes are boggy. They are often found near rivers and on badly drained high ground.

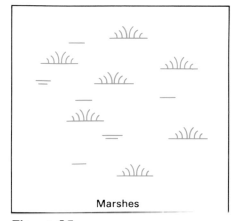

Marshes

Figure 25

7 Revision map 2

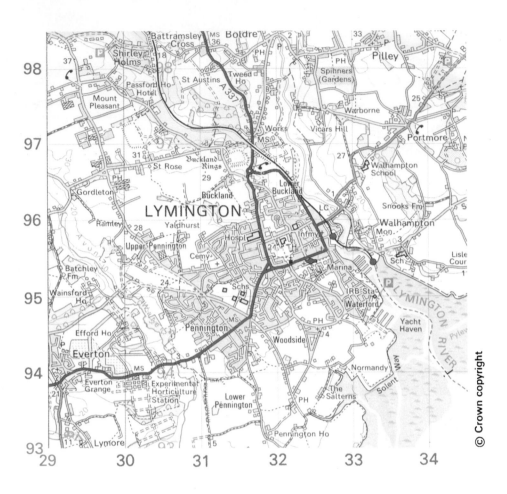

1. How can you tell that farming takes place in square 2996?
2. In what way are the trees near the main road in square 2994 different from those in other parts of this square?
3. Name three important public buildings in the town of Lymington.
4. Why is sailing difficult in square 3393?
5. In what way is the church at 333983 different from that at 322955?
6. Give six figure grid references for **a** a post office, **b** a public house and **c** a mile stone.
7. What is the general direction of the secondary road in square 2993 (e.g. north-south or east-west)?
8. A grid square has an area of one square kilometre. What is the approximate area shown by the map? What do you think is the area of the town of Lymington?
9. Why do you think there are no buildings along the coast in the southern part of the map?
10. There is plenty of woodland in square 3094 but there is very little in the adjoining square (3194). Can you think of a reason why?

8 The shape of the land

A map is drawn on a flat piece of paper. However, land is rarely perfectly flat. For this reason special symbols have been invented to show height.

The most important of these symbols is the **contour line**. Contour lines join places which are the same height above sea level.

Figure 1

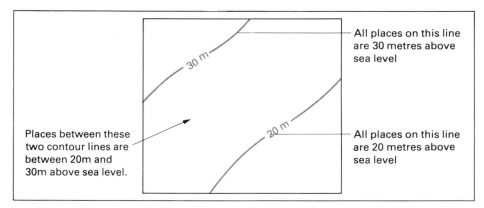

All places on this line are 30 metres above sea level

Places between these two contour lines are between 20m and 30m above sea level.

All places on this line are 20 metres above sea level

Some contours may be close together while others are further apart. However, the difference in height between each contour line on a map is always the same. On metric 1:50 000 maps this difference is 10m.

Figure 2

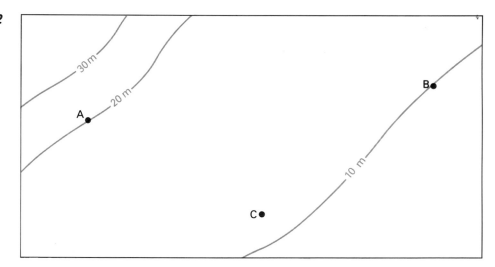

1 Look at Figure 2 and then copy the following sentences, choosing the correct answer from inside the brackets.

A is (20m 30m) above sea level.
B is (10m 20m) above sea level.
C is between 20m and (10m 15m) above sea level.

2 Copy Figure 2 into your exercise book and draw an arrow across it to show which way the land is rising.

The heights of certain places not on contour lines are also shown on Ordnance Survey maps. They are shown by **spot heights** and **triangulation points**. Very accurate measurements of heights have been made by the Ordnance Survey at these places.

Figure 3

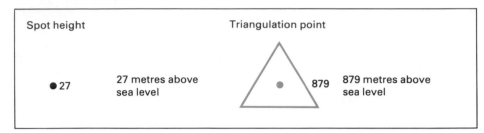

On flat areas where contour lines are far apart spot heights are very useful. Slight changes of height can be very important in such areas.

Figure 4

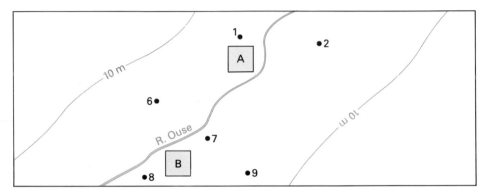

3 Figure 4 shows two farms, marked A and B. Which farm is likely to suffer more from flooding?

Figure 5

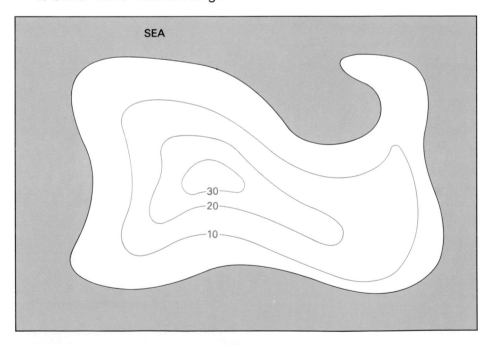

4 Draw those parts of the island in Figure 5 which will still be dry land if the sea level rises by **a** 10m, and **b** 20m.
5 On your first island put in a spot height at 18m and a triangulation point at 36m.

Slopes

Contour lines do not only show the height of the land. They also show its shape and the way it slopes. The closer together the contour lines, the steeper the slope. The further apart the contour lines, the gentler the slope.

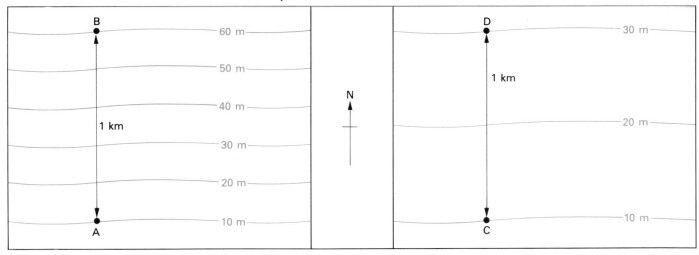

Figure 6a

b

In Figure 6a the land between A and B rises 50m in 1km. In Figure 6b the land between C and D only rises 20m and 1km.

6 On which diagram is the slope steeper?
7 Copy out the following paragraph and fill in the blanks.

Naina walked from A to B. She walked _____ km and climbed from 10m above sea level to _____ m. Her friend Sam walked from C to D. Sam also walked 1km but his walk was much _____. Both friends walked in a _____ direction.

Figure 7

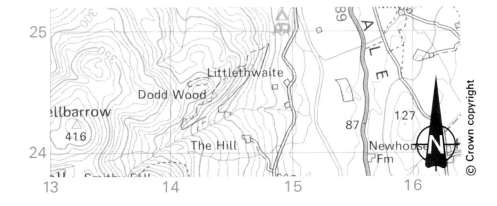

8 In which square are the slopes gentlest?
9 Why do you think the secondary and minor roads are on the eastern side of this map?
10 What is the height of the secondary road at 156243?
11 What is the height of the triangulation point at the **summit** (top) of Fellbarrow?
12 Name two other places where height has been accurately measured by the Ordnance Survey.

Valleys and spurs

When a river flows over the land's surface it cuts a **valley** for itself. In all river valleys the land rises on either side of the river. Sometimes the land rises sharply while at other times the slopes are quite gentle.

Figure 8

The lowest land in a valley is always found by the river itself. It is also at the river that the contour line for any particular height extends furthest inland. Where it crosses the river it makes a sort of V shape. The tip of the V always points up the valley towards higher land.

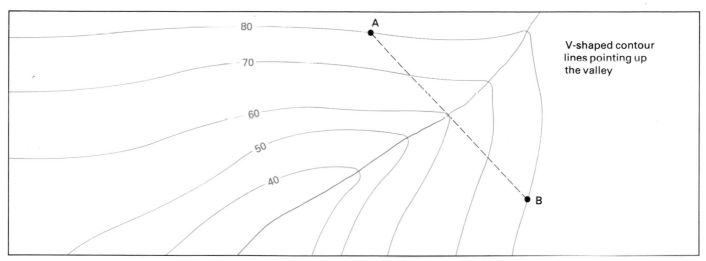

Figure 9

13 Imagine you walked across this valley along the straight line between A and B.
   a What height did you start walking from?
   b At what height were you when you reached the river?
   c Why was the second part of your journey from the river to B more tiring?

It is possible to show the shape of the valley by drawing a cross-section. Take a straight edged piece of paper and place it along the line marked A–B. Mark off the heights of the contours as shown in the diagram.

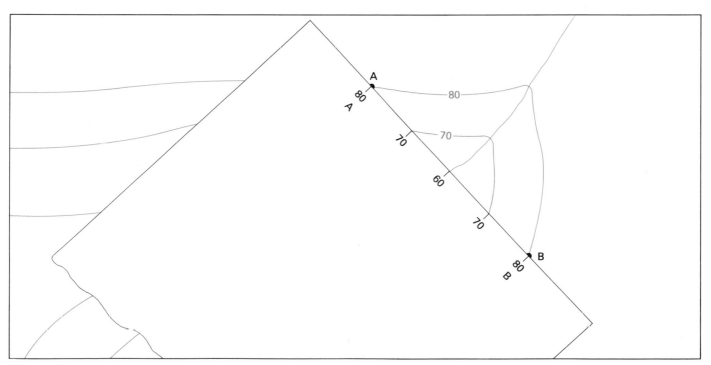

Figure 10

Now draw the base of your cross-section into your exercise book. It must be the same distance (A–B). The sides of the cross-section will show the height above sea level.

Figure 11

Match the A–B on your piece of paper with the base you have just drawn. Using your paper as a guide, place dots at the correct height on your cross-section. This is shown in Figure 12.

Figure 12

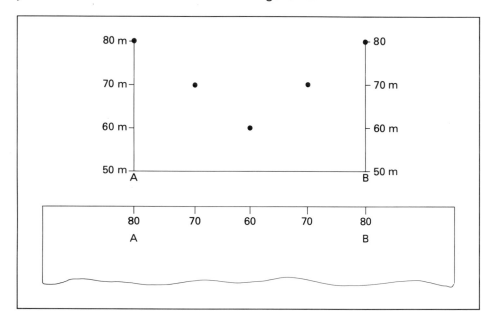

When you have joined all the dots you will have completed your cross-section. It should look like this.

Figure 13

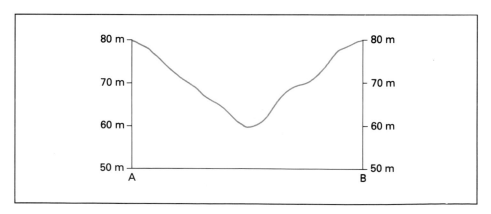

14 Shade in your cross-section to show the land area.
15 Print 'A cross-section of a river valley' as a title to your cross-section.
16 Place a letter R to show where the river is.

Figure 14 shows a piece of upland extending into the valley. This is called a **spur**. The contours for a spur are more rounded and can be described as U-shaped.

Figure 14

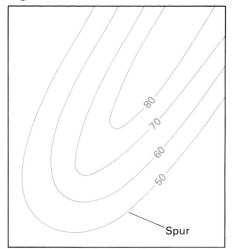

This time the contours are pointing towards lower land.

Figure 15

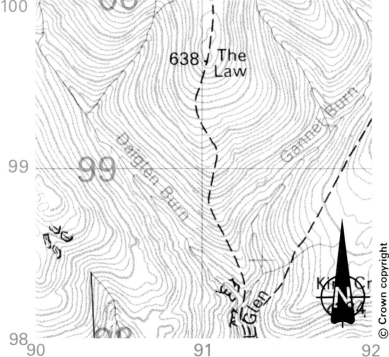

© Crown copyright

Several valleys containing streams can be seen on the Ordnance Survey map.

17 What are the names of the two largest streams?

18 How can you tell that there is a spur between these two streams.

19 Are the slopes of this spur steep or gentle?

20 Copy out the following sentences choosing the correct words in the brackets.

The Daiglen Burn flows (slowly/quickly) from (south-east/north-west) to (south-east/north-west). The sides of this valley are (steep/gentle).

9 Industry

There is no special symbol on Ordnance Survey maps to show industry. However, since industries usually have large buildings, they tend to stand out anyway. Sometimes words are added to describe the type of industry which takes place in these buildings. Often just **Works** or **Factory** will be printed alongside the building symbol. In the case of a mine, the word **Mine** or **Colliery** is used.

Factories often group together. This is called an **Industrial Estate** and is again printed on the map.

Figure 1

Industries need transport and power. Large works dealing with bulky products have freight lines. These bring in raw materials and take out finished products. Most factories in industrial estates are small and produce 'light' products, such as pens, shoes or watches.

All factories need power and this is supplied by electricity transmission lines.

1 Look at Figure 1 then name the type of transport mainly used by such small factories.

Figure 2

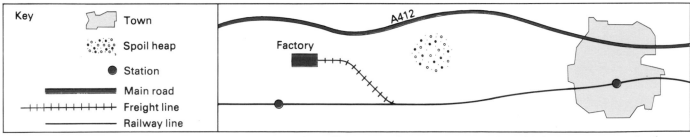

Key

Town
Spoil heap
Station
Main road
Freight line
Railway line

2 Look at Figure 2. State two ways in which the workers in the factory can get to work.
3 How can you tell that the factory uses the railway to transport goods?
4 Why might the people living in the town be unhappy with this factory?

The Ordnance Survey map shows an industrial area at the mouth of the River Tees.

Figure 3

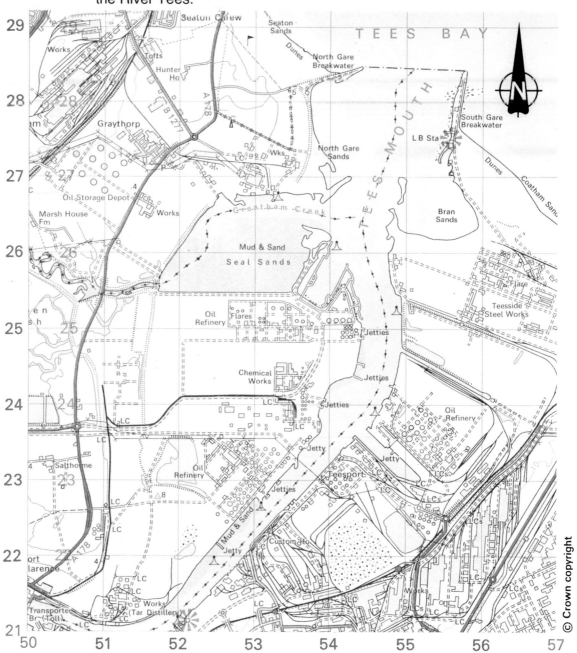

© Crown copyright

5 Look at Figure 3 and name three different products made in this area.

6 Large oil tankers sail along this part of the River Tees. What has been built to allow these heavy ships to dock in deeper water away from the river bank?

7 How can you tell that the harbour in square 5423 is human made?

8 Why are there so many railway lines in square 5028?

9 If you looked west from the railway station at 549218, you would not have a pleasant view. Why not?

10 Where else on this map would you see similar sights?

11 Why do you think there are no houses in the area around Seal Sands?

12 How can you tell that the works at 528271 use a great deal of electricity?

13 Industry often needs large quantities of water. Where might the works in 5521 get its supply from?

10 Past Peoples

Thousands of years ago, Britain looked very different from how it does today. There were no factories or farms, no roads or railways and no towns. On the lowlands the land was often marshy and covered with thick forest. The forest was dark and contained many wild, dangerous animals.

Figure 1

1 Look at the drawing and give three reasons to explain why few people lived on the lowlands.

Most people lived in small settlements on the hills. The land there was drier and not so forested. The soil was lighter and much easier to plough than the soil of the marshy lowlands. The word 𝕮𝖆𝖒𝖕 is used by the Ordnance Survey to show the location of such simple settlements. 𝕯𝖎𝖙𝖈𝖍𝖊𝖘 were often dug around the camps to make them easier to defend. For the same reason, camps were often built on mounds or 𝕰𝖒𝖇𝖆𝖓𝖐𝖒𝖊𝖓𝖙𝖘.

Often all that remains today are the burial places of these ancient Britons. These are shown on Ordnance Survey maps by the words 𝖇𝖆𝖗𝖗𝖔𝖜, 𝖈𝖆𝖎𝖗𝖓 or 𝖙𝖚𝖒𝖚𝖑𝖚𝖘. (The plural of tumulus is 𝖙𝖚𝖒𝖚𝖑𝖎.)

Wherever they could these people farmed the land in a simple way. Figure 2 shows what such farmed land looks like today.

Figure 2

On Ordnance Survey maps such land is labelled 𝔣𝔦𝔢𝔩𝔡 𝔰𝔶𝔰𝔱𝔢𝔪.

These ancient Britons built some large circles of stone blocks which may well have been used as places of worship. The word 𝔠𝔦𝔯𝔠𝔩𝔢 locates their remains.

Figure 3

The terms used so far have been written in **Gothic** print. All words dealing with people who lived in Britain before the Romans came are printed in this way.

Figure 4

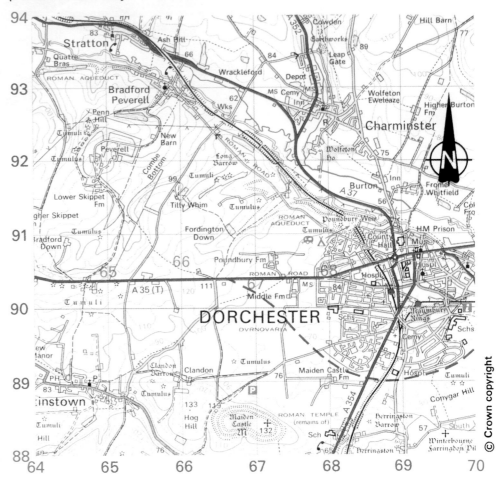

2 What is the name of the ancient settlement to the north-west of Dorchester?

3 Name two types of burial ground found in square 6691.

4 As well as words, a symbol may be used to show a burial ground. Draw this symbol into your exercise book.

5 Why are none of these symbols to be found on the low land near the River Frome?

The Romans began their conquest of Britain in 55 BC (that is 55 years before Christ was born). They finally left four and a half centuries later. During their stay, the Romans built **camps** and **forts** to house their soliders. These were connected to each other by a system of roads. Roman roads were very well built and some parts of them can still be seen today.

The Romans were skilful craftsmen and constructed large, beautiful **villas** like the one in Figure 5.

Figure 5

Important citizens, such as governors, lived in these villas. The Romans also designed centrally heated pools called **baths**.

Many Roman remains have been found in the Dorchester area shown in Figure 4.

6 Look at square 6789 and find out the Roman name for Dorchester
7 Which modern road follows the course of the old Roman road west of Dorchester? (Give its A-number).
8 How would you describe this road?
9 The A354 also follows an old Roman road. Why might you have guessed this?
10 In what way is the printing used for Roman remains different from that showing the remains of early man?

The remains of historical buildings built after the Romans left our shores are also shown on Ordnance Survey maps. They include religous buildings such as cathedrals, abbeys and monasteries, and the castles around which many towns grew. Rich landowners lived in large manor houses.

11 Look at the Dorchester map and name the castle to the south-west of the town.
12 Why was this castle built on a hill?
13 What is the name of the manor house in square 6892?

Such remains are called **post-Roman** because they were built after the Romans. Those of the ancient Britons are called **pre-Roman** ('pre' means before).

As you can see from this diagram, both pre and post Roman terms are shown in Gothic print.

14 Copy Figure 6 into your exercise book and complete the blanks.
15 Look at the map of Dorchester again then try to add more words to each list.

Figure 6

Barrow	PRE ROMAN
Cairn	
C _ _ l _ _	
C _ _ p	
Di _ _ _	
C _ _ _ _ _	55 B.C.
Road	ROMAN
V _ _ _ a	
B _ _ _ s	
Fort	
C _ _ p	
	400 A.D.
Manor House	POST ROMAN
C _ _ _ _ _ ral	
C _ _ _ l _	
A _ _ _ v	
m _ _ ast _ _ _	
	PRESENT DAY

11 Villages and towns

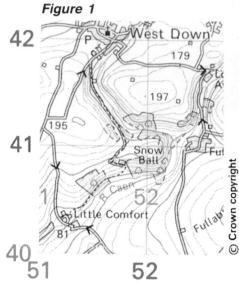

Figure 1

The Ordnance Survey map Figure 1 shows the **village** of West Down. Villages are usually quite small and therefore contain few **services**. Services include shops, banks, schools, hospitals, etc. They are facilities that people can make use of. In a small village like West Down it may be that only one or two shops, a public house and a primary school are needed. The small number of people living in villages means that traffic is slight. For this reason main roads and railway lines are less common than in towns and cities.

1 Name one of West Down's services that is shown on the map.
2 Ordnance Survey maps do not show every service. Name two services that are not on the map but are probably found in West Down.
3 What type of road runs through West Down?

Towns are usually much larger than villages. For this reason they contain far more services. There may be a shopping centre, council offices, secondary schools, hospitals, etc. Main roads and railways are also found in towns. This is well illustrated by the Ordnance Survey map of Salisbury shown below.

Figure 2

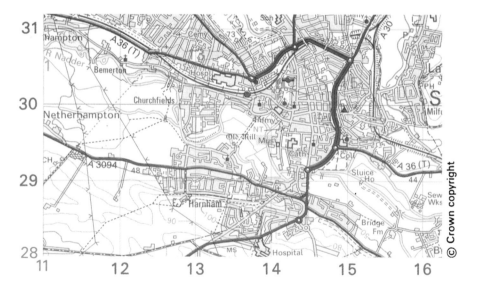

4 What are the numbers of the three main roads that pass through Salisbury?
5 As you can see from the map Salisbury contains far more services than the village of West Down. Name four of these services.
6 These services are not used only by the people of Salisbury. People from the surrounding area also make use of them. Imagine you lived in the village of Netherhampton (1129). Give a six figure grid reference where you would:
   a Catch a train to London.
   b Have your tonsils taken out.
   c Meet your cousin who has travelled by coach from Scotland.
7 State two ways that Netherhampton and West Down are similar.

12 Scale

Figure 1 is a map of a classroom.

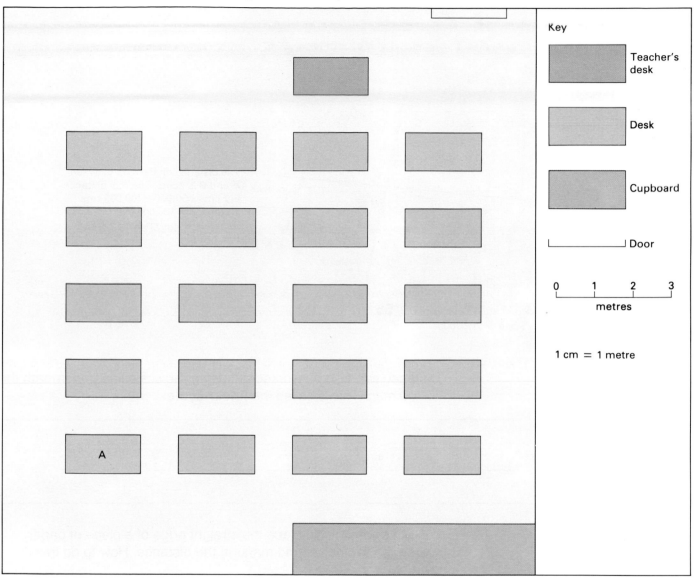

Figure 1

Distances between points on this map are much less than the actual distance in the classroom. The desks in the map, for example, are only 1cm apart. The actual distance between these desks is 1m. This was worked out by using the **scale** given beside the map. As you can see the scale of the classroom map is 1 cm = 1m This means that every centimetre on the map is equal to a metre in the real classroom.

1   Use the scale underneath the key to find the length of **a** the teacher's desk, **b** the cupboard, and **c** the side wall.
2   Could an average twelve year old sitting at desk A touch the wall with their hand?
3   Make a simple scale drawing of your classroom.

Figure 2 is an Ordnance Survey map. The scale of this map is 1:50 000. This means that every centimetre on this map is equal to 50 000 centimetres on the Earth's surface.

Figure 2

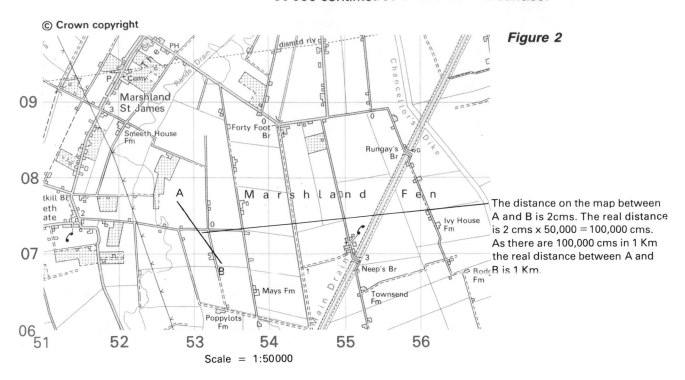

The distance on the map between A and B is 2cms. The real distance is 2 cms × 50,000 = 100,000 cms. As there are 100,000 cms in 1 Km the real distance between A and B is 1 Km.

Scale = 1:50000

Distance can also be worked out using the scale line underneath the 1:50 000 map. This is called the **linear scale**.

Figure 3

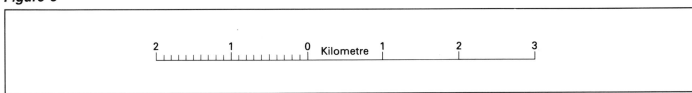

To use this linear scale place the straight edge of a piece of paper between the two points and mark off the distance. How to do this is shown below.

Figure 4

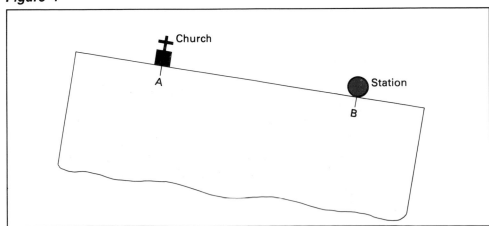

Now place the piece of paper along the linear scale. Make sure you line up the first point with the zero on the scale. The distance in kilometres can now be read off.

Figure 5

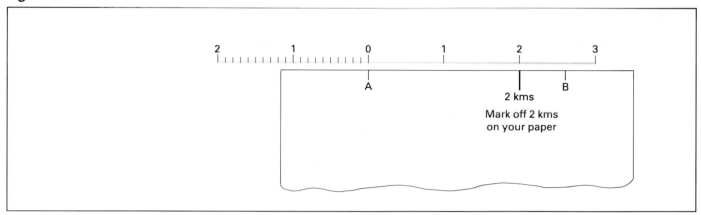

The remaining distance is now placed along the far left of the scale where each small line is equal to 100m.

Figure 6

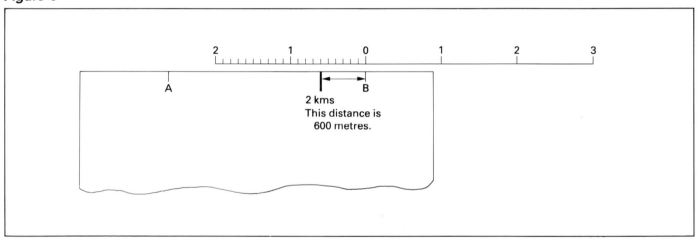

As you can see the remaining distance is 600m. This means the actual distance between the church and the station is 2km 600m (2.6km).

Look at the Ordnance Survey map (Figure 2) and answer the following questions.

4   A boat race started at Rungay's Bridge (558083) and finished at Neep's Bridge (551069). How far did the competitors row?
5   The County Council has decided to improve the surface of the minor road that runs from the building at (547087) to Neep's Bridge. The cost is £5000 per kilometre. What will be the cost of improving this section of road?

13 Revision map 3

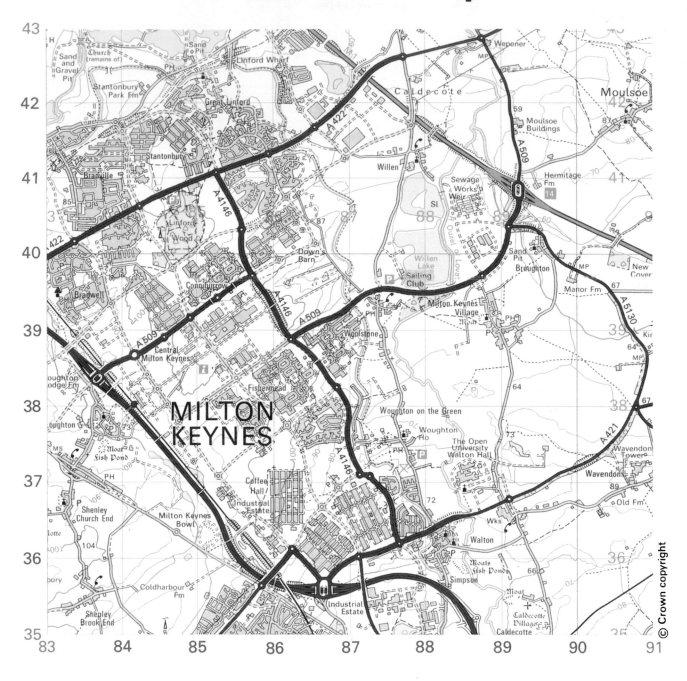

© Crown copyright

1. At which junction would motorists leave the M1 to travel to Milton Keynes?
2. How can you tell that Milton Keynes village (8839) is an old settlement?
3. Give the grid reference for another old settlement on this map. What is its name?
4. Give two reasons why you think the industrial estate in square 8636 is in a good position.